Nourishing Connections

Like a wild flower discovered in a field of wheat, poetry captures a distilled significance. Graham Kings' poems celebrate the intimacies and the immensities of his faith and the world, as well as the love which connects them, and they point us towards the beauty we might have too easily have passed by.

Mark Oakley, Dean of St John's College, Cambridge and author of The Splash of Words

Seamus Heaney said that good poetry offers 'phrases that feed the soul'. Graham Kings' *Nourishing Connections* is full of rich and memorable phrases that do indeed nourish the soul and make fresh and illuminating connections for the mind. It is a collection that will reward close reading and slow savouring.

Malcolm Guite, poet, singer-songwriter and author of Sounding the Seasons

Above all, there is a biblical imagination at work and play, generating connections in all directions – past, present and future. And, as with any meaning thoroughly rooted in the Bible, there is a combination of tough truth and God-centred encouragement.

David F. Ford, Regius Professor of Divinity Emeritus, University of Cambridge

Luminous and evocative poems that focus issues raised by lives both modern and biblical in a way that no prose ever could. They will accompany many people fruitfully on their journey of faith.

John Barton, Emeritus Oriel & Laing Professor of the Interpretation of Holy Scripture, University of Oxford

Graham Kings' exquisitely constructed début as a poet does indeed nourish connections, integrating the scope and depth of his experience as a bishop with a profound devotion to tradition and literature. His poems range in form from the pithy and playful to a prose poem, as fusing the biblical with the contemporary, he is for us 'replaying memory and pattern of promise'.

Micheal O'Siadhail poet and author of The Five Quintets

Attentive to the providential word play of language and the lyric charms of rhythm, rhyme and repetition, Graham Kings' poems are meditations for a spirit-hungry modern generation. Take one a day to chew, absorb and digest.

Dr Jennifer Wallace, Harris Fellow and Director of Studies in English, Peterhouse, University of Cambridge.

Erudite and often international in its concerns, yet always accessible for a lover of poetry, Graham Kings' poems display depth and devotional energy in ways that bring to mind the best religious poets of our day. It is a book you will want to share with the people who mean the most in your life.

A M Juster is a prize-winning American poet and is Poetry Editor of First Things

Nourishing Connections

Poems

Graham Kings

CANTERBURY
PRESS
Norwich

First published in 2020 by Canterbury Press Norwich
Editorial office
3rd Floor, Invicta House
108–114 Golden Lane
London EC1Y 0TG, UK

www.canterburypress.co.uk

Canterbury Press is an imprint of
Hymns Ancient & Modern Ltd (a registered charity)

H
Y Ancient
M &Modern
N
S

Hymns Ancient & Modern® is a registered trademark of
Hymns Ancient & Modern Ltd
13A Hellesdon Park Road, Norwich,
Norfolk NR6 5DR, UK

British Library Cataloguing in Publication data

A catalogue record for this book is available
from the British Library

978 1 786 22277 0

Typeset by Regent Typesetting
Printed and bound in Great Britain by
CPI Group (UK) Ltd

Contents

For Ali

Preface

Many of these poems emanate from meditation on passages of the Bible, which have nourished me over the years, and from connections across the world, especially in the Anglican Communion.

Commentators in the early and medieval Church used the language of digestion and nourishment to refer to meditation on Scripture, especially the sound of the words. The Latin words *ruminare* and *mundicare* refer to a cow chewing the cud and they resonate across the centuries as we pray that we may 'read, mark, learn and inwardly digest' God's holy Word.[1]

Robert Atwell, Bishop of Exeter, has commented:

Our forebears' belief that the slow digestive process of cows was well-suited to describe the process of engaging with Scripture stands in marked contrast to the language and expectations of a fast-food generation. Their wisdom calls us to a more gentle rhythm of prayerful reading in which patience, silence and receptivity are vital ingredients.[2]

1 Collect for 'Bible Sunday', the Second Sunday in Advent in the Book of Common Prayer and the Last Sunday after Trinity in *Common Worship*.

2 Robert Atwell (ed.), *Celebrating the Seasons: Daily Spiritual Readings for the Christian Year* (Norwich: Canterbury Press, 1999), p. v.

Poetry involves playing with words seriously and some-times with a light touch. Alliteration, assonance, rhythm and rhyme all make connections across the traditions, place, space and years.

Favourite poets of mine, who enjoyed puns, riddles and acrostics, include St Aldhelm, first Bishop of Sherborne (705–9 AD); Hrabanus Maurus, Archbishop of Mainz;[3] George Herbert and Samuel T. Coleridge.

In the Holy Scriptures, nourishing meanings are often drawn out by wordplay.

Isaiah of Jerusalem prophesies (Isaiah 5.7):

[God] expected justice (*mishpat*),
　　but saw bloodshed (*mispach*);
righteousness (*tzedakah*),
　　but heard a cry (*tz'acha*)!

Jesus connects the name he gave to Simon, *Cephas*, which means 'rock' in Aramaic, as *Petros*, does in Greek, with his wider purpose:

And I tell you, you are Peter, and on this rock I will build my church, and the gates of Hades shall not prevail against it.
(Matthew 16.18)

Paul plays on the name of the runaway slave, Onesimus, which means useful, with his aim of returning him to Philemon, his brother in Christ:

---

3 Hrabanus Maurus wrote the Latin poem *Veni Creator Spiritus*, which was translated for the 1662 Book of Common Prayer by John Cosin, Bishop of Durham, as 'Come Holy Ghost our Souls Inspire' and is sung at the ordination of priests and consecration of bishops.

Formerly he was useless to you, but now he is indeed
useful to you and to me.
(Philemon 11)

In Ephesians 4.16, Paul writes of the body of Christ in
terms of nourishing connections:

> But speaking the truth in love, we must grow up in
> every way into him who is the head, into Christ, from
> whom the whole body, joined and knitted together by
> every ligament with which it is equipped, as each part
> is working properly, promotes the body's growth in
> building itself up in love.

Ruminations reverberate around the world. As a family
we have lived in London, Kenya, Yale in the USA, Cam-
bridge and Dorset, and I owe a debt of gratitude to many
young, emerging theologians whom I have met in these
and other places, especially in the global South of the
Anglican Communion.

I give thanks to God for the vibrancy of the art of
Silvia Dimitrova, the Bulgarian Orthodox icon writer and
painter based at Downside School, Somerset. Our 17-year
project together of 'Women in the Bible' is now complete.
Many thanks also to Tristan Latchford, for his seven
anthems based on Sylvia's paintings and on my poems.

Christine Smith, commissioning editor of Canterbury
Press, has given encouraging and nurturing insight for
both Signs and Seasons (2008) and for this collection
of poetry. Martin Brasier's design for the accompanying
website, Nourishing Connections (www.grahamkings.
org), is lucidly beautiful, and Natalie Sloan's photographs
are scintillating. I am very grateful.

I thank God for the joy and support of my beloved family: Kathleen and Ralph (parents, whose faces are reflected in the Sarah painting on the inside front cover); Ali (wife and muse for 43 years); Rosalind, Miriam and Katie-Wambui (daughters); Jon, Munene and Solomon (sons-in-law); and our grandchildren.

List of illustrations

SEASONS

Christmas

The Gospel of the Song

In the beginning were the Words,
  and the Words were the Poet's,
  and were part of Him:
  lively and brilliant.

And the Words became music,
  and were sung,
  full of beauty and freedom.

We have heard the Song,
  and been utterly moved,
  again and again.

We had read poetry before,
  but beauty and freedom
  came through this Song.

No one has ever seen the Poet:
  this one Song, which is in His heart,
  has shown Him to us.

Matter of Great Moment

For God, matter matters:
For the Word became flesh.

In the beginning was the Meaning,
And the Meaning became matter,
And the matter became moment,
And the moment became movement,
And the Meaning moved us.

For God, matter matters:
For the Word became flesh.

The Ultimate Became Intimate

God became poor,
God plumbed the depths,
God used body language,
God used means to save mean people,
God came as a foreigner to earth for our benefit,
God crossed the widest cultural chasm in the cosmos.

Meaning became matter in a moment,
Matter became movement,
Meaning moved us,
Matter matters for God,
For the Ultimate became intimate.

A Cord

One accord for all
between
God and woman:
according to his word,
God becomes
conceivably small.
Life-giving cord
is cut for life:
Heir of the world
gulps
air of the world.

The Nativity

Mary was led out of Nazareth,
for her protection from prying eyes,
as her waist grew,
to stay with Elizabeth
for promise fulfilment
and peaceful pondering.

Mary was led out of Nazareth,
for her protection from flying stones,
as the day drew near,
to travel with Joseph
for Bethlehem's promise
and painful birth.

Mary was led out of Bethlehem,
for their protection from piercing swords,
as her son grew,
to live in Egypt:
replaying memory
and pattern of promise.

Epiphany: Magi Momentum

Farcical Journey

Persians not Arabs,
Farsi not Arabic,
Magi not Kings,
Worship not rule.

Crazy and farcical,
Leaving two rivers,
To follow a star,
To worship a King,
A journey afar.

Leaving behind
Family and kin,
Like Abram of old,
Unlike the King,
Outside his line.

Through Centuries

From the beginning,
Magi pondered and travelled;
    offered and worshipped.

For the record,
Matthew collected taxes and stories;
    scribed and described.

In the sermon,
Lancelot Andrewes translated and prayed;
    preached for the King.

Through the poem,
T. S. Eliot essayed and imagined;
    journeyed to Christ.

Feigning Faith

Herod the King,
   Racially Arab,
   religiously Jewish,
   culturally Greek,
   politically Roman.

Baffled, bewildered
   by naïve strangers,
Shocked and scared
   by sacred page.
Secretly, exactly,
   gathers facts,
   feigns faith,
   requests report:
Diligent intelligence.

Offerings Presented

Away from home,
Mission accomplished:
It is finished.

Star trek over,
King discovered,
But not as they know it.

Rapturous joy,
Offerings unwrapped.

Mined mineral, for brilliant mind;
Sweet savour, for sense of spirit;
Balm of burial, for enwrapped body.

Warned and turned,
They follow the Way:
Another way home.

We Refugees

By the first dream,
    I was assured:
Mary was faithful,
    Not fooling around.
That was fulfilled.

By the second dream,
    I was warned:
We three refugees
    Needed to flee.
This was frightening.

We took the road South,
To Gentile territory,
    Terrified.
Oppressive or safe?
Who could tell?

Sad and miserable,
    Sleepless nights,
Hungry and thirsty,
    On the move,
Hardships, distress.

How can we sing
    The Lord's song
    In a strange land?
How long, O Lord?

Owning nothing,
    Yet, with this child,
    Possessing everything.

Terror Unleashed

Outwitted, outmanoeuvred,
 Herod unleashes terror.

Revenge, outraged, ventures out,
 Unresisted, unrestrained.

Many are slaughtered to slay the One:
 The One survives to save the many.

Perennial Problem

Into Egypt,
    Joseph was sold,
    rose to the heights,
    and saved my people.

Out of Egypt,
    Moses was freed,
    received my Law,
    and led my people.

Out of Egypt,
    I called my Son,
    brought by family,
    renewing my people.

Threat of death passed over,
    bypassing Judea,
    Galilee beckons,
    Nazareth welcomes,
    my Refugee.

Tragically, later,
    home town rejects
    home-grown Prophet,
    who cites my acts
    for people outside.

Unsightly reaction incited:
    my perennial problem.

Holy Week and Easter

Gethsemane and the Trinity

Conflict is stranger than fiction;
Love is stronger than faction;
God is no stranger to conflict.

God is stranger than we know,
stronger than we feel,
weaker than we think,
wider than we imagine.

The cup of Gethsemane
is the cup of the Trinity.

The Hostage Deal

Between the rolling of the stone
  and the crying of the name
  came the agonizing.

Shuddering, Jesus stares into the tomb,
Making a deal with death in the depths.
A greedy exchange is strangely agreed:
Lazarus comes out and he will go in,
The prize of life for the price of death.

The hour of starkness fully come,
The Dealer is struck and laid in the tomb.
Then is the end, but the end is of death:
Through terrifying life in the depths,
Death is destroyed, exploded inside.

Before the rolling of the stone
  and the coming of the women
  came the rising.

Hooked

The great fish vomits Lazarus:
Jaws of Death, with bated breath,
Await the Lord of heaven and earth –
   And that's the catch.

But who is caught?
Life is swallowed up in death:
Death is hooked, wound up, wound in,
   And that's the end of him.

Easter Prayer

Lord Jesus Christ,
we follow in your trail,
   blazing through life;
we sail in your wake,
   surging through death;
we are your body,
   you are our head;
ablaze with life,
   awake from the dead.

Finished in the New Creation

The flourishing hand of Bach,
interweaving the sum of his works,
leaves unfinished
his Art of Fugue,
interrupted, solely,
by the glory of God.

The measureless hand of Coleridge,
dreaming an early work,
leaves unfinished
his Kubla Khan,
interrupted, perhaps,
by the person from Porlock.

The impressive hand of Turner,
evoking multiple works,
leaves unfinished
his paintings in progress,
interrupting exhibits
by adding light touches.

All are finished, completed, perfected,
in the new creation of God.

Pentecost

The Image of Her Father

For many years in Israel's womb
The embryo grows, the Church of Christ:
First the Head, then the Body,
The Son of Man includes the many.

For hours upon a Roman cross
The Church's birth begins in blood:
Crucified with Christ her Head,
Constricted by the love of God.

The third day, from a gaping tomb,
The Church emerges urgently:
Risen again with Christ her life,
Released, relieved, the joy of God.

The fiftieth day, with tongues of flame,
She breathes the Spirit, cries the word:
Conceived, inspired with Christ, she grows,
The heir of all, the child of God.

Pentecost Prose Poem

It seems to me that the Holy Spirit may appropriately be called 'He' or 'She' but not 'It', for the Spirit is profoundly personal, not a simple force. For a change, let's try 'She'.

She bubbles like a spring, tumbles like a waterfall, meanders like a river and welcomes us like the sea. You may as well try to bottle the wind as capture her. She is wild and unrestrained, surprising and unpredictable, yet true to her character and utterly reliable. She is reticent and reflective, giving glory to the Son and the Father.

Like the wild desert wind she drives and scorches. Like the oil of the olive tree she heals and soothes. In a still, small voice she speaks and questions. The contemptuous proud she resists and brings down. The humble poor she supports and uplifts. Our imagination she enlarges and stretches. Our humdrum existence she enlightens and enlivens. Who can resist the draw of her calling to come to Christ and delight in God?

She does not force and manipulate, but coaxes and draws. She inspires, enthuses, interprets and invigorates. She warns and reminds, convicts and convinces. She brings joy and delight, depth and sorrow, a feast in want and fasting in plenty.

She does not ingratiate but delivers grace. She does not calculate but risks adventure. She does not rest on her heels but is fleet of foot. She is not sedentary but agile, not ponderous but quicksilver. All who know her, love her, for she loves the Son and the Father.

Holy Spirit: Remembrancer

O Holy Spirit, Giver of Life,
Illumine my sin,
Which lurks and creeps in darkness:
Give me your life,
Which swirls and leads into light.

O Holy Spirit, Inspirer of Languages,
Release my tongue
From cynical cursing,
To praise you, Father and Son,
With eloquent wisdom.

O Holy Spirit, Remembrancer,
Refresh my memory,
With words of Moses and Jesus,
To help me follow your ways
And imagine your future.

O Holy Spirit,
Cascading water, coursing down the mountainside,
Whirling wind, sweeping up the valley,
Flaming fire, crackling in the hearth,
Soothing oil, seeping into cracks in an old cricket bat,
Fill me.

PEOPLE

Turning Point: Augustine

Give me chastity and continence, but not yet.
(Augustine, *Confessions* VIII, 7)

Put on the Lord Jesus Christ, and make no provision for
the flesh, to gratify its desires.
(Romans 13.14)

Stalking in the garden in the heat of the moment,
Reflecting on complexity of voluntary movement,
Slunk in listless and leaden despair,
Tangled, contorted and tearing his hair,
Rapping his head and wrapping his knees,
Rabidly ravaging under the trees,
Wanting to wait and waiting to want,
Weighing the longing of laying and font,
Augustine hears the Word of the Lord
Drifting, insisting the voice of a child:
'*Tolle, lege*: take it and read.
Tolle, lege: take it and read.'
Vocative discourse spoken by God,
Evocative sing-song challenge of a child.

Turning and turning he opens to read
The Word of the Lord in the words of St Paul:
'Lust and debauchery, revelry, rivalry,
Now is the time to wake from your sleep.'
Eloquent professor professes his call.

Now, no procrastination, delay;
Later is now, tomorrow today.

Beyond Imagining: Mandela

Before nineteen eighty six,
theology in the Reformed Church
was mistakenly myth-taken,
double Dutch and in a State.

People on whom God had set his stamp
were stamped upon;
That which God had joined together,
man put asunder.

Then came pressure from the Spirit
through the Word,
through the people,
through the nations.

Abusing the image insults the Original;
That which man had kept
apart, tied
together now by God.

February nineteen ninety:
behold the man,
whose image froze
a generation ago.
Has he changed? Will we know him?
President elect, but for election!

Here they come! Which one is he?
The one with Winnie's hand
in his left,
saluting the crowd
with the fist of his right.

The image and likeness of the Creator,
oppressed in black, distorted in white;
The image of a captured lawyer,
stamped on T-shirts for the fight;
now the release of a camera shutter,
captures the image of a regal elder –
reproduced in black and white.

Prophet: Bishop Muge

On Saturday a Minister of State in Kenya
threatened a Minister of God in public,
if he or his colleague entered his kingdom:
'They would see fire
and may not leave alive.'

On Tuesday, the prophet,
impatient, impulsive,
pugnacious, courageous,
insisted on seeking the kingdom of God
and on his right to preach in Busia.

Triumphal entry and service over,
on returning, he returned Home.
The unmarked lorry, released from a police check,
headlights blazing – mid-afternoon –
cut in, cut up, cut off Bishop Muge.

The Minister of State resigned,
   but boasted of his prophecy;
the driver went to prison,
   seven years for dangerous driving;
the people talked of murder,
   the Party's over.
'Après moi, le déluge.'

*Bishop Alexander Muge was the Anglican Bishop of
Eldoret in Kenya; he died in Busia on 14 August 1990.*

Thanksgiving: Bishop John V. Taylor

What tears are these that run down cheeks unchecked?

For a burning star in the African sky
    and the Anglican firmament;
For a personal poet of go-between theology;
For a passionate lover of God, of Peggy,
    of art and of Africa;

For his visionary insight into meetings
    of politics, faith and ecology;
For his drawing delight in producing plays
    in Uganda and Winchester;
For his spiritual reflection of our missionary God
    in the face of Jesus Christ.

What tears are these that run down cheeks unchecked?

Tears of joyful anointing and missing mission;
Tears of thanks, for giving to me
    encouraging depth, writing and blessing.

A Prior Meeting: Anselm

Solvitur ambulando
around the 'cloister' meadow
of Grey Friars, Canterbury.

Five days in Bec, Normandy,
now, beckoned and called,
four days, silent, in Canterbury.

Cassock forgotten,
now vested from the vestry,
a gift, it turns out, from Bec.

'Something-than-which-
nothing-greater-can-be-conceived'
is God.

Quite a thought from Anselm,
a Prior and Abbot of Bec
and Archbishop of Canterbury,
echoing around the cloister
and through the centuries.

God cannot be thought of
as non-existent
without contradiction.

It seems too neat:
perfectly to define God,
in effect,
with the property of existence.
Kant couldn't.

If conception is not earthed
is it real?

God was conceived and earthed
in Nazareth.

Maybe 'meeting' is the clue
    which coheres?
The co-inherent meeting,
    of Father, Son and Holy Spirit,
    of Word and flesh,
    of God and people.

'Someone-than-whom-
no-one-greater-can-be-met'
is God.

So, God-who-meets is
co-inherent not incoherent,
and cannot not be met.

Hail God, well met.
Quite an adventure,
coming across God,
in the meadow,
in the cool of the evening.

Visit of Holiness: Rowan

Only God is holy,
Father, Son and Holy Spirit.

So any holiness we see,
and experience in anyone,
is God's own holiness,
shining out in God's own child.

Of what does it consist?
Humility, profundity and silence.

Humility comes from the ground,
from being earthed in 'humus':
from dust we come and
to dust we shall return.

But the earth is the Lord's
and everything in it.
So even being earthed
is being rooted in God.

Humility is the pattern of Christ,
   the shape of the Spirit,
      the mould of God.

Humility is attractive, a focus of God.
We are drawn in, delighted:
our petty selves are drawn out, transformed.

Profundity comes from the sea:
Out of the depths I cry to you, O Lord.
It also comes from way back, from afar,
from long-past vocations and foundations,
from the wisdom of God and language of learning.

Out of the depths of
Hebrew Scriptures, Greek Gospels,
Church fathers and mothers of all ages,
We cry to you, O Lord.

Silence echoes the stars:
In returning and rest we are saved,
in quietness and trust is our strength.
For God alone our souls wait in silence.
We have calmed and quieted ourselves,
like a weaned child with its mother.

Silence brings
peace amidst chatter;
stillness amongst clatter;
essence at the end of incessance;
space for God's eloquence.

Three Popes

Karol Wojtyla: Polish Pope

A poem written on the day of his funeral

In St Peter's Square,
Presidents and Prime Ministers,
Princes and people gather.
A simple cypress-wood coffin
Is surmounted by the gospel book.
He said he lived his life
Under the word of God.
The ruffling wind of the Spirit
Bears witness, turning its pages.

A previous Pope,
John the Twenty-Third,
The great caretaker,
In surprising wisdom
Opened the windows of the office.
The rushing wind of the Spirit
Blew piles of paper in the air,
Upturning, updating, unfolding
The Church.

John Paul the Second,
The great survivor
Of Nazi invasion and
Communist constriction.
The poet and playwright,
Priest and professor:
Polish Pope.

In theology:
Restressing of tradition,
Regression of liberation,
Redressing of primacy.

In politics:
Solidity of Petrine rock,
Solidarity of Polish stock,
Stumbling of Soviet bloc.

Karol Wojtyla,
More alive than ever,
Witness to the watching world.

Joseph Ratzinger: European Pope

In St Peter's Square,
Holy smoke and a shy smile
Of Bavarian piety and curial power.

Funeral oration,
Conclave sermon,
Acceptance address:
Momentous momentum.

A hard act to follow,
They chose a hard man.
In thinking, penetrative;
In doctrine, conservative;
In power, effective;
In discipline, pressive:
Continuity reigns.

Enforcer becomes caretaker
To take care of Europe;
Lost continent, now
The option for mission;
Postmodern, enlarging,
Deserting tradition.

Joseph Ratzinger:
Perhaps, for some time,
Last Pope from Europe.
Africa, Latin America,
Burgeon and beckon.

A conservative caretaker,
Astounded the sixties:
May Benedict the Sixteenth
Surprise us with blessing.

Jorge Bergoglio: Latin American Pope

In Saint Peter's Square:
'*Buona sera.*' 'Good evening.'
From the ends of the world,
a friendly greeting, typical of Saint Francis.

Connecting identities:
Italian parentage, Argentine heritage;
Jesuit order, Franciscan humility.

In Buenos Aires:
limousine and palace were left on the wayside,
for bus and flat, with people on the wayside.

For the Conclave:
Latin America beckons,
and bequeaths a Pope.
In Rome:
periphery becomes central,
Papacy becomes simpler,
Curia become curiouser.

May Francis the First
open the windows of the Church
for fair winds of the Spirit.

PLACES

Gallery into Oratory

East Gallery, Bishop's Palace, Wells;
windows of light, in and on three walls.

At the previous evening's preview,
people gathered without gathering,
and looked without seeing.

In the peace of a fresh morning,
the gallery becomes oratory,
flowing with your presence.

I bring a chair to sit
and gaze, amazed, at you,
the Saviour and Giver of Life.

I peer through wood and tempera
to you, the Peerless One.
You see through my appearances,
and pierce flesh and temperament.

Your right hand gives
the sign of bread and blessing;
your left hand holds
the Word of life and love.

To you, I give thanks for saving me;
to you, I turn and return my life.

Though icons are unsigned,
Silvia's love for you
shines through and through.

She is the woman who
wipes the hair of her brush
on your face and neck,
your hands and garments,
pouring out her life.

Signing the invoice,
my inner voice sighs:
Pearl without Price,
owning nothing, I owe everything
to you, the Only One.

Through the abundance of your face,
flow the subtleties of your grace,
knowing, guiding, anointing,
searching, guarding, sending.

Jesus Goes Underground

She listens to her Walkman
    living in another world,
      ignoring her neighbour as herself.

He reads *The Sun*
    immersed in actors' lives,
      washing his mind with soap.

They do not touch,
    insulated, isolated,
      marriage withdrawal symptoms.

She scrunches monster munches,
    monosodium glutamate;
      bags of tasty emptiness.

He's stuck in sniffing glue,
    addicted to cheap death;
      nobody knows the trouble he's in.

To bring them to their senses and together,
    Jesus goes Underground.

He grabs the tube of glue
    and breathes the breath of God.

He throws the packet away
    and gives her bread.

He joins their hands in his
    and brings them warmth.

He folds *The Sun* in half
   and beams a smile.

He slips the headphones from her ears
   and shares his news.

Pillar in Poets' Corner

Perched on a pillar
in Poets' Corner,
gazing upwards,
not looking down
on his critical friend,
is S. T. Coleridge.

At the foot of the pillar,
stowed beneath,
naturally pondering,
prelude to writing,
one leg crossed,
head inclined,
sits William Wordsworth.

A gap between them,
opposed in elevation,
intimations of intimacy,
intense and tense,
taught and distraught:
remembered here,
they share a pillar.

Is Jesus the Son of *Allah*?

Kneeling alone on the soft carpet
of a Mombasa mosque,
chandeliers above, galleries around,
stereo system stacked high in the corner,
the quiet question came to me –
is Jesus the Son of *Allah*?

The question is not about Jesus, but *Allah*:
The Arabic for God is more than a name
but is He the same
as our God and Father?

In Southern Sudan
a Christian will answer, militantly, 'No':
In Pakistan
a Christian may answer, philosophically, 'Yes':
In Saudi Arabia
a Muslim will answer, immediately, 'No':
So does it depend where we stand – or kneel?

El Shaddai of Abraham
Is revealed as *Yahweh* to Moses,
But not as *Ba'al* to Elijah:
What of 'Almighty Allah'?

The crucial clue may lead us to
A Muslim now submitting
To the Ultimate Submitter,
Jesus the Messiah.

He does not change his God,
for God is One,
But discovers in the Son
That God is strangely, inconceivably great,
because He became so conceivably small;
That God, in the end, is mercifully just
since He has absorbed the evil of all.

We may, perhaps, then whisper
that Jesus is the Son of *Allah*:
But in this naked act of naming,
the active Word transforms the Name.

Prostrate upon the carpet of a Mombasa mosque,
Softly to Jesus, Son of *Allah*, I prayed;
Then rose again to slip outside
and join my wife and daughters,
who were waiting in the shade.

Meandering in South Sudan

From southern equatorial mountains,
and eastern ancient highlands,
to northern Mediterranean Sea,
through four nations, till recently,
and now through five,
the Nile passes without passport.

She flows onwards and downwards,
with gravity and delight,
imperturbably, irresistibly, ineluctably,
circumambulating
with gesticulating grace.

Last week, in blazing dusty Malakal,
I stood on the east bank, near thin cattle,
gazing at the setting sun,
reflected in the river
touching the west bank,
undeveloped for millennial miles and years.

This evening, in hot and green Juba,
I sit on the west bank, near portly cows,
looking east at lush trees,
across the drifting river,
meditating through millennia.

Among the bulrushes of Egypt,
a baby is hidden for safety,
and discovered by royalty,
for raising and releasing of Israel.

Near the banks of the Nile,
a baby is saved from Israel,
for refuge, return and royalty:
'Out of Egypt have I called my Son.'

BIBLE

First Written Gospel

Jesus the Sacred, tried before Pilate;
Pilate, the scared – trial before Caesar?
Jesus, entitled to justice from Rome,
entitled by Pilate, 'The King of the Jews'.

First written Gospel, translated for all,
title deeds of the kingdom of God;
proclaimed to the city, unchanging Word,
'What is written, is written', bequeathed to the world.

Six Poems on Luke

Profit and Loss

Luke 3.2–18

John is just the right man for the job,
which is, after all,
one of justice and righteousness.

Savile Row clothes aren't suitable,
nor is aftershave;
the dust and smell of the desert
hang about him;
so do the people.

The word of the Lord,
silent for so long,
at last is heard again:
'It's time to change!'

Not a polite call, in this waste land,
of 'Time, gentlemen, please';
not 'Time to leave
for tomorrow is another day'
– for it probably isn't!

But 'The crisis has come.
This is it. Here is he
who comes after me.'

Not 'You can't change the world,
that's just the way it is.'
But the specific question,
'Is it just, the way it is?'

The health of the poor in Britain rots
– improve housing and benefits;
The hunger and debt of the world mounts
– trade fairly and justly;
The inside of the stock market collapses
– deal honestly and openly;
Stars Wars astronomically cost the earth
– be content with present defence.

His shout demands, 'Time to change,
turn around, you can't go on.'
Not a casual 'Take it or leave it'
But a crucial 'Take it or be left'
– like the chaff.

'And don't you try the old school tie;
Trees are judged by fruits, not roots.'

Revolutionary Love

Luke 6.20–36

Turning the world upside down
is the charge against Silas and Paul:
turning its values the right way up
is the kingdom's promise and call.

Invitations to a glorious feast
mean more to the hungry and poor,
and to others who have the least,
than to the rich, well known and well fed,
who prefer their own company instead.

Cathedral sermons attack terrorism
but are preached under
fading regimental flags of
former colonial glory.

This kingdom sermon counters violence with love
and is preached under
the regimental rule of
imperial Rome.

Revenge surrenders to evil
by reflecting violence:
but, like a bad coin kept
and not passed on;
like lightning conducted
safely to earth,
love neutralizes evil
by absorbing violence.

Love for those who like you is
    ordinary;
Love for those who are like you,
    narcissistic;
Love for those who are unlike you,
    extraordinary;
Love for those who dislike you,
    revolutionary.

Pray for the rival who threatens you;
Pray for the adversary blocking you;
Pray for the opponent who slanders you;
Pray for the antagonist provoking you.

You only love the Father
as much as you love
your worst enemy.

For your love is to be
merciful and free,
indiscriminate, spontaneous,
uncalculatingly generous;
When all is said and done –
like Father, like Son.

Combines or Labourers?

Luke 10.1–12

The world isn't won
With church statistics
 on compact discs,
With escapist, bright,
 free offers,
 vacuum-packed,
 market-researched,
 Teflon-coated,
 via satellite.

Jesus sends us out
Without this gear:
Not to make the gospel easy,
Just to make it clear.

He sends not combine harvesters
But only his own labourers,
 poor and vulnerable,
 weak, dependent,
 humbly serving,
 healing, preaching.

'Believe it or not,
Like it or not,
The kingdom's come.
For the King has come;
A reign of peace,
Or sentence of doom.'

The Resistance Movement

Luke 13.18–21

Ask for a clear definition,
he'll reply with a story or two;
Not what the kingdom is,
but what it's likened to.

It all begins so small,
Yet ends up being tall;
It starts by being hidden,
and ends when all is risen.

In a Galilean synagogue,
  a Jewish rabbi
    heals the crippled and weak;
In a Wittenberg study,
  a German monk
    wrestles with Romans in Greek;
In an Alabama bus,
  a black woman
    sticks to her white-reserved seat;
In a Calcutta slum,
  an Albanian nun
    nurses a beggar in the street.

The seed is sown,
fermenting begun;
though hardly known,
the kingdom has come.

Yet it is not complete:
so discern and trace
What is going on
in what is taking place.

The Cost of Living

Luke 18.18–30

In the world, the ruler can buy his own way
with influence, riches and law:
for the kingdom, the cost is too high to pay –
joining the life of God's poor.

Trust and interest in temporary wealth
do infinite damage to eternal health:
Trust in the King, interest in the poor,
make future heavenly treasure sure.

The rising cost of living,
solidarity and care,
means the only rule for giving
is 'more than you can spare'.

But just when you reckon
the rich are so depraved
and, possessed by their possession,
they're unable to be saved,
right through the needle's eye
Zacchaeus gallops apace.

As much as you may try,
there's no accounting for grace.

The Point of the Nails

Luke 23.26–47; 24.45–48

Sins aren't erased
by a finger
pushing the cancel button:
they're absorbed
by a body
pushed around and broken.

Surrounded by
mocking curiosity,
derisive frivolity,
vindictive invective,
Jesus dies,
declared innocent by
governor, criminal and soldier.

As bread is his body
and wine is his blood,
he, King of the Jews,
is his people.

His death crowns their pain
under pagan regimes:
he is smashed for their sins
and the nations' gain.

He is raised with a transformed body,
not as a flimsy ghost;
not like a thin carbon-copy,
nor even the original
returned in the post.

He is raised to glorious new life,
not back into the same,
not like Lazarus his friend
who has to die again.

As the Jews were his crucified flesh,
so the Church is his glorified body.

ART

Tender Attention

Mother's head is
lightly inclined;
baby's body is
safe and special,
sound and secure,
encircled, enfolded,
enwrapped, embraced:
welcome wonderful world.

Women in the Bible

Sarah

'Look to the rock from which you were hewn,
    and to the quarry from which you were dug.
Look to Abraham your father
    and to Sarah who bore you.'
(Isaiah 51.1–2)

Who is this woman,
Eyes uplifted,
Elderly, beautiful,
Pondering, anxious,
Right hand responsive,
Stopping laughing,
Brow furrowed,
Fingers knobbly,
Left hand supportive,
Relaxed, accepting?

Who is this man,
Eyebrows surprised,
Mature, elegant,
Wondering, welcoming,
Left hand cupped
Near to heart,
Beckoning hearth,
Reckoned as righteous,
Right hand blessing,
Thickening calf?

Who are these visitors,
Arrayed in radiance,
Mysterious in difference,
Framed by bowing
Oaks of Mamre and
Tent of Meeting,
Together as three,
Emerging out of
Scintillating leaves
Merging as One?

Mother of Promise
Of people and nations,
Forever empty,
Who ceased to be
After manner of women,
Laughs to herself,
Then covers it up,
Eventually conceives,
Bears and believes
'He who laughs'.

Father of Promise
Of people and nations,
As good as dead,
Who previously laughed,
Suggesting a son of
Slave girl instead,
Now furnishes
Nourishing relief,
Hope against hope,
Sealing belief.

Lord of Promise
Of people and nations,
Proclaiming astonishing
Fertility, fecundity,
Wonderfully righting
Wrongful response:
For incoherent jest,
Co-inherence sows.
From mature oaks,
An acorn grows.

Miriam

Who is this woman,
Tapping a tabor,
Rejoicing in song,
Elegant in beauty,
More than Egyptian?

Who is this baby,
Lifting his limbs,
Drifting in basket,
Floating on river,
Secluded in reeds?

Who are these men,
Walking together,
Bearing symbols,
Leading the way
Between fire and water?

Miriam, the prophet,
The shrewd saviour
Of baby brother,
Dancing, proclaims:
'Sing to the Lord
Who has triumphed gloriously;
Horse and rider,
He has thrown into the sea.'

Moses, on the Nile,
Escapes annihilation,
Responds at bush of fire,
Foils Pharaoh's ire,
Receives the Law in awe,
Accompanies Aaron, the eloquent,
Whose head and beard and robe
Will run with precious oil.

The Red Sea is redressed:
Waves of horses crest the waves,
Roaring, rushing, downing, drowning,
Trampling hostile oppression.

For God's people, safely across,
Good things come to those who wait.

Ruth

Who is this woman,
Poised and balanced,
Pointing to baby,
Carrying sheaves, which
Wave to waves of barley?

Who is this man,
Supporting, protecting,
Prosperous, assured,
Backed by sprouting
And spreading tree?

Who is this madonna,
Cuddling a boy,
With delight and tenderness,
Signalling the way
To fertile foliage?

Ruth, the Moabite,
Widowed, bereaved,
Loyal and faithful to
Mother-in-law from Israel.

'Where you go, I will go:
Where you lodge, I will lodge:
Your people shall be my people
And your God, my God.
Where you die, I will die
And there will I be buried.'

Ruth reaps and gleans
A harvest of love
And husband of joy.

Boaz, worthy and wealthy,
Honourable and wise,
Hospitable to foreigner,
Welcoming, redeeming,
Redresses history
And Moses in Moab.

Naomi, triply emptied,
Gentle guidance
Now fulfilled,
Nurses her grandson.

Obed, gurgling, worshipping,
Bequeaths the tree of Jesse.
Bethlehem rejoices to house
The house of David,
And, in God's good time,
Great David's greater son.

Esther

Who is this woman,
Framed by arches,
Beautiful, bountiful,
Centred, subtle, shrewd,
Carrying scented lilies?

Who is this man,
Pictured with pillars,
Royal, imperial,
Majestic, magnetic,
Extending his sceptre?

Who is this man,
Holding a scroll, eyes alert,
Beckoning, suggesting,
Suppliant, petitioning?

Who is this man,
Head down, eyes closed,
Gallowed, glowering,
Schemer, scowling?

Who are these girls,
Gazing at us,
And the woman,
With posy and scroll?

Esther, Jewish Queen of Persia,
Orphaned, adopted, awesome,
Raised to the heights,
Reticent, persuasive, risk-taker,
'If I perish, I perish',
Bravely delivers her race,
From depths of death.

Xerxes, King of Persian Empire,
Reigns in citadel of Susa,
From India to Ethiopia,
Opulent, hospitable, terrifying,
Saved by Esther from murder,
Hears her pleas for her people.

Mordecai, cousin of Esther,
Foster-father, chronicler,
Honourably perceptive:
'Perhaps you have come
To royal dignity
For such a time as this?'

Haman, vizier of Xerxes,
Machiavellian murderer,
Plans destruction of Jews:
Snarler ensnared,
Worsted, reversed, hoisted,
Despised for ever.

Children and families,
Throughout the ages,
Celebrate Purim,
Reading the scroll,
Feasting and sharing,
Remembering friendship and revenge.

Yet, the Jew of Nazareth
Enjoins love for enemies,
Endures imperial gallows,
Absorbing vengeance:
Death is destroyed by
Esther's successor at Easter.

Magdalene

Who is this woman facing this man,
Head lightly inclined,
Eyes wide open, gazing;
Hands uplifted, palms upward, surprised;
Gorgeously arrayed?

Who is this man facing this woman,
Coming from the right,
Profile clear, bearded;
Hand outstretched, palm down;
Gloriously apparelled?

Behind her, two angels hover,
Reflecting her shape:
Behind him, scented trees lean,
Setting the scene:
Below her, a dark opening hints.
All silent witnesses.

The eyes have it:
Focus of tension and attention.
One word awakes her: 'Mary'.
One word responds: 'Rabbouni'.

Their hands shape a triangle
At the centre of meeting:
Her two, shocked and suppliant;
His one, blessing, calming, sending.

Lydia

Who is this woman,
Slender in purple,
Approaching the river,
Head demure,
Hands across
Heart secure?

Who are these women,
Accompanying her,
Tumbling, cascading,
Following her gaze,
Slightly perplexed,
Subtly amazed?

Who is this man,
Bearded, intriguing,
Joining the women,
Gorgeous in vesture,
Gently announcing
Greeting in gesture?

By the river of Philippi,
They sat down and met
And sang the songs of Zion,
Outside the gate of the
Greek city, Roman colony.

Lydia, with friends and household,
Dealer in purple, in business astute,
From Thyatira in Asia Minor,
Gentile worshipping God of the Jews.

Paul, with friends, Silas and Luke,
Following a vision of Asia Minor,
Meets a woman of Macedonia,
The good news comes to Europa.

With hearts open to the cross of Christ,
They pass through the river of baptism,
To enter the joy of the kingdom.
Like trees planted by the waterside,
They bring forth their fruit in due season.

Priscilla

Who is this woman,
Pure eyes, profoundly rounded,
Beautiful face, honourably tilted,
Open hands releasing dove?

Who is this man,
Noble head, bearded attractive,
Working hands, intently attentive.
Inclined together, touching love?

Who are these men,
Weighing a letter, ponderingly,
Carrying a scroll, inscrutably,
Trees and windows hovering above?

Four converge on Ephesus,
Silver shrine of Artemis,
Expound the word of God
And form a church at home in love.

Priscilla and Aquila,
Refugees from Roman Emperor,
Host to Paul at Corinth and Ephesus,
Fellow workers in Christ and canvas,
More accurately explain the Way
To the Jew of Alexandria.

Apollos, eloquent and scriptural,
Burning and enthusing,
Knowing now the Holy Spirit,
Crosses over to Corinth
And causes chaos. Perhaps
Composes letter to Hebrews?

Paul writes to church at Corinth,
Settling contending leaders.
Paul sows, Apollos waters,
God gives the growth.
Ironically, rhetorically,
Cross empties eloquence.

Priscilla and Aquila return to Rome,
Hosting the body of Christ in their home.

PRAYER

Prayer Stool

I leave aside my shoes, my ambitions;
undo my watch, my timetable;
take off my glasses, my views;
unclip my pen, my work;
put down my keys, my security;
to be alone with you, the only true God.
　　　After being with you,
I take up my shoes to walk in your ways;
strap on my watch to live in your time;
put on my glasses to look at your world;
clip on my pen to write up your thoughts;
pick up my keys to open your doors.

The Pause

Sentences, like people,
need spaces to breathe.
Between the full stop
and the Capital
lies the pause.

Without the space,
sentences are breathless;
without the Sabbath,
life is restless;
without the pause,
the rest is lifeless.

Sentences, like God,
have a preferential option
for the pause.

Prayer and God

The Foolishness of God

For God's foolishness is wiser than human wisdom,
and God's weakness is stronger than human strength.
(1 Corinthians 1.25)

Our Father,
you are great and glorious;
but to this twisted world
your wisdom and power
seem stupid and feeble:
grant us your insight,
your subtlety and love,
to show you to people
as you really are,
focused in your Son,
Jesus Christ our Lord,
Amen.

The Kingdom of God

'The time is fulfilled, and the kingdom of God has come
near; repent, and believe in the good news.'
(Mark 1.15)

Our Father,
You are for turning;
turning us round,
　　upside down,
　　inside out;
help us to give ourselves
to your revolution of
challenge and love,
through him who called for
turning and trust,
Jesus Christ our Lord,
Amen.

The Strangeness of God

For the LORD will rise up as on Mount Perazim,
he will rage as in the valley of Gibeon
to do his deed – strange is his deed! –
and to work his work – alien is his work!
(Isaiah 28.21)

Our Father,
you are a wild God,
   yet we try to tame you;
you exiled your people,
   gave up your Son,
   raised up a convict,
   for our welcome home:
you are a free God,
   yet we try to cage you.

The Maturity of God

> When they had finished breakfast, Jesus said to Simon Peter, 'Simon son of John, do you love me more than these?' He said to him, 'Yes, Lord; you know that I love you.' Jesus said to him, 'Feed my lambs.'
> (John 21.15)

Father,
Draw us to maturity
    by the training of your Spirit,
Lead us in your love
    by the example of your Son,
      from sentimentality to compassion,
      from propaganda to evangelism,
      from hurry to urgency,
      from presumption to assurance,
      from optimism to hope,
Through Jesus Christ our Lord. Amen

Boat Prayer

Lord Jesus Christ,
teacher on the shore,
    who calls and overwhelms us,
friend in the boat,
    who sleeps and saves us,
mystery on the water,
    who prays and surprises us,
stranger on the other shore,
    who rises to welcome us,
guide our boat across.

By the Waters of Delivery

By breathing and brooding,
by breaking and birthing,
by parting and loosing,
by stirring and soothing:

by giving, re-living,
by stilling, refreshing,
by drowning, immersing,
by raising, re-versing,

you, Lord, deliver us.

Litanies

Bible Litany

In the beginning was the Word.

God spoke his word through Abraham and Moses,
Deborah and Hannah,
Samuel and David,
Isaiah, Zechariah.
It is written — it is written,
And the Word became flesh.

God spoke his word through
Mary and Elizabeth,
Simeon and Anna,
Peter and Paul,
Matthew and Johanna.
It is written — it is written.

God speaks his word in
Urdu and Tamil,
Xhosa and Hausa,
Spanish and English,
Mandarin and Maori.
It is read — it is read.

In the beginning was the Word,
And the Word became flesh.

It is written, it is read;
It is old, it is new;
It is God's, it is true.

Likeness Litany

Formed in the image and likeness of God,
   We rejoice;
Fired by violence and facing away,
   We recoil;
Defaced, despairing, curved in on ourselves,
   We cry;
Remaking, repairing, curved into the world,
   You come, the Image of God.

With compassion, forgiveness, restoring the image,
   You heal;
With powerfully piercing, incisive insight,
   You teach;
With passion and proverb and practical story,
   You preach.

Facing Jerusalem, challenging temple,
   You suffer;
Surfacing from the depths of death,
   You're raised;
Infusing, renewing, the image refacing,
   You pour out the fiery Spirit of God.

Being transfigured into your likeness,
   From glory to glory;
With unveiled face, we face God's Image,
   Reflecting the light of the knowledge of God,
   Seen in your face,
   Jesus our Lord.

Pentecost Litany

God the Father forms his people,
   from out of the nations to bless the nations;
Jesus the Christ saves his people,
   from out of the nations to bless the nations;
The Holy Spirit draws his people,
   from out of the nations to bless the nations.

Abraham called,
   from out of the nations, the people are blessed;
Moses leads,
   from out of a nation, a people oppressed;
David fights,
   against the nations, the people assured;
Isaiah speaks,
   to lighten the nations, the people restored.

Jesus dies,
   betrayed by the people, for the people;
Jesus dies,
   pierced by the nations, for the nations.

Jesus raised,
   the people remade, the nations reproached;
Paul proclaims,
   the people reshaped, the nations rejoice;
John sees,
   **the people redeemed, regathered from every
tribe, tongue, people and nation.**

Source of the Church,
   Desire of the nations;
Head of the Church,
   Judge of the nations;
Breath of the Church,
   Light of the nations;
Father, Son and Holy Spirit,
   renew your Church to bless your nations.

Trinity Litany

In the beginning, mission in communion:
The Father sent the Son and the Spirit.

God spoke his word through
Melchizedek and Hagar,
Rahab and Ruth,
Balaam and Naaman,
Jethro and Job.

Together they are sent:
Together we are sent.

God spoke his word through
Woman of Samaria,
Roman soldier,
Woman of Phoenicia,
Caesarea centurion.

Together they are sent:
Together we are sent.

God spoke his word through
Monica of Africa,
Ajayi Crowther,
Abdul Masih,
Pandita Ramabai,
Watchman Nee.

Together they are sent:
Together we are sent.

From the beginning, mission in communion.
'The Father sent me: I send you.'
Receive the Spirit:
the Spirit of release.

Until the end, Holy Communion.
Our hearts are fed, by Christ by faith,
We proclaim his death, until he comes.

Maranatha, Alleluia: Alleluia, Amen.
Maranatha, Alleluia: Alleluia, Amen.

Acknowledgements and Notes

Grateful acknowledgement is made to the editors and publishers of the following books, journals, magazines and websites in and on which these poems were first published.

The Gospel of the Song – first published in *Christian*, January 1990 and in Mission Theological Advisory Group, Anne Richards (ed.), *Transparencies: Pictures of Mission Through Prayer and Reflection* (Churches Together in Britain and Ireland (CTBI) and Church House Publishing, 2002), as well as in Graham Kings, *Signs and Seasons: A Guide for Your Christian Journey* (Canterbury Press, 2008) and also on the *Spiritual Journeys* and *Fulcrum* websites (www. spiritualjourneys.org.uk; www.fulcrum-anglican.org. uk).

Matter of Great Moment – first published on *Fulcrum*, December 2005, then in Kings, *Signs and Seasons* and also on *Spiritual Journeys* and *Covenant*, the weblog of the Living Church Foundation (https://livingchurch. org/covenant).

The Ultimate Became Intimate – first published on *Fulcrum*, December 2014.

A Cord – first published on *Fulcrum*, December 2012.

The Nativity – first published on *Fulcrum*, December 2010 and on *Spiritual Journeys*.

Farcical Journey – commissioned and first published in Andrew Wheeler, *Desire of the Nations: The Magi, their Journey and the Child* (Seimos Press, 2015) and on *Covenant*, January 2016.

Through Centuries – as above.

Feigning Faith – as above.

Offerings Presented – as above.

We Refugees – as above.

Terror Unleashed – as above.

Perennial Problem – as above.

Gethsemane and the Trinity – first published on *Fulcrum*, April 2012.

The Hostage Deal – first published in *The Christian Century* 110.11 (April 1993), then in Kings, *Signs and Seasons* and on *Spiritual Journeys*.

Hooked – unpublished.

Easter Prayer – first published in Kings, *Signs and Seasons* and on *Spiritual Journeys*.

Finished in the New Creation – first published on *Fulcrum*, April 2010 and on *Spiritual Journeys*.

The Image of Her Father – first published in *International Review of Mission* LXXX.317, January 1991, in Kings, *Signs and Seasons* and on *Spiritual Journeys*.

Pentecost Prose Poem – first published in Kings, *Signs and Seasons* and on *Fulcrum* and *Spiritual Journeys*.

Holy Spirit: Remembrancer – first published on *Covenant*, October 2017 and on *Spiritual Journeys*.

Turning Point: Augustine – first published in Richards, *Transparencies*, in Kings, *Signs and Seasons* and on *Fulcrum*, December 2013 and *Covenant*.

Beyond Imagining: Mandela – first published in

Transformation: An International Journal of Holistic Studies 7.3 (July 1990) and on *Spiritual Journeys*. For the photograph of Nelson and Winnie Mandela, see www.grahamkings.org.

Prophet: Bishop Muge – first published in *Theology* 120.4 (July/August 2017).

Thanksgiving: Bishop John V. Taylor – published on *Spiritual Journeys*.

A Prior Meeting: Anselm – first published on *Fulcrum*, August 2010, on *Spiritual Journeys* and in Graham Kings, 'Remembering, Thinking, Imagining: Augustine, Anselm and Rowan' on *Covenant*, June 2018.

Visit of Holiness: Rowan – first published on *Fulcrum*, December 2012 and on *Spiritual Journeys*.

Karol Wojtyla: Polish Pope – first published on *Fulcrum*, April 2005, on *Spiritual Journeys* and on the London Diocesan website.

Joseph Ratzinger: European Pope – first published on *Fulcrum*, April 2005.

Jorge Bergoglio: Latin American Pope – first published on *Fulcrum*, March 2013.

Gallery into Oratory – first published on *Fulcrum*, September 2007, in Kings, *Signs and Seasons* and on *Covenant* and *Spiritual Journeys*. For a photograph of the icon *Jesus, Saviour and Giver of Life* by Silva Dimitrova, see www.grahamkings.org.

Jesus goes Underground – first published in Richards, *Transparencies*.

Pillar in Poets' Corner – first published in *Theology* 120.4 (July/August 2017).

Is Jesus the Son of *Allah*? – first published in *International Bulletin of Missionary Research* 14.1 (January 1990), then in Kings, *Signs and Seasons*.

Meandering in South Sudan – first published on *Fulcrum*, February 2013.

First Written Gospel – first published in Richards, *Transparencies*, Kings, *Signs and Seasons*, on *Fulcrum*, April 2009, in *Mission Studies* 16.2 (1999), and on *Spiritual Journeys*.

Profit and Loss – first published in Richards, *Transparencies*.

Revolutionary Love – first published in Richards, *Transparencies*.

Combines or Labourers? – first published in *International Review of Mission* LXXVII.308, October 1988.

Resistance Movement – first published on *Mission Theology in the Anglican Communion*, January 2017 (www.missiontheologyanglican.org).

The Cost of Living – first published in *Theology* 120.4 (July/August 2017).

The Point of the Nails – first published on *Fulcrum*, April 2014 and on *Spiritual Journeys*.

Tender Attention – first published on *Fulcrum*, December 2008 and on *Spiritual Journeys*, and based on a sculpture I bought in the Dom Kerk, Utrecht, by an unknown sculptor (see www.grahamkings.org).

Sarah – first published on *Covenant*, June 2016 and on *Mission Theology in the Anglican Communion*.

Miriam – first published on *Covenant*, September 2018.

Ruth – first published on *Covenant*, July 2019.

Esther – first published on *Covenant*, February 2019.

Magdalene – first published as 'Rabbouni' on *Fulcrum*, September 2007, in Anne Richards with Mission Theology Advisory Group, *Sense Making Faith: Body, Spirit, Journey* (CTBI, 2007), in Kings, *Signs and*

Seasons and on *Covenant, Spiritual Journeys, Mission Theology in the Anglican Communion.*

Lydia – first published on *Covenant*, June 2016 and on *Mission Theology in the Anglican Communion.*

Priscilla – first published on *Covenant*, June 2016 and on *Mission Theology in the Anglican Communion.*

The Prayer Stool – first published in J. Robertson (ed.), *A Touch of Flame: Contemporary Christian Poetry* (Lion, 1990), on *Spiritual Journeys* and republished in several magazines and websites.

The Pause – first published on *Fulcrum*, March 2007 and on *Spiritual Journeys.*

The Foolishness of God – first published in the Church Missionary Society *Prayer Paper*, 1987 and in Richards, *Transparencies.*

The Kingdom of God – first published in the CMS *Prayer Paper*, 1987 and in Richards, *Transparencies.*

The Strangeness of God – first published in the CMS *Prayer Paper*, 1987 and in Richards, *Transparencies.*

The Maturity of God – first published in the worship booklet of the 1989 San Antonio Conference of the Council for World Mission and Evangelism of the World Council of Churches.

Boat Prayer – first published in Richards, *Transparencies.*

By the Waters of Delivery – first published in Richards, *Transparencies* and Kings, *Signs and Seasons.*

Bible Litany – first published as 'Canterbury Rap' in *News of Liturgy*, 1993, then in John Stott et al., *The Anglican Communion and Scripture* (Regnum Books, 1996) and on *Fulcrum, Spiritual Journeys* and *Mission Theology in the Anglican Communion.*

Likeness Litany – first published as 'Facing the Image' in *News of Liturgy*, 1997, *Transformation* 15.1 (1998),

Richards, *Transparencies* and on *Fulcrum*, *Spiritual Journeys* and *Mission Theology in the Anglican Communion*.

Pentecost Litany – first published as 'The Church and the Nations' in *News of Liturgy*, 1995, *EFAC Bulletin*, on *Fulcrum* and on *Spiritual Journeys* and *Mission Theology in the Anglican Communion*.

Trinity Litany – first published as 'Limuru Litany' on *Fulcrum*, June 2014 and on *Spiritual Journeys* and *Mission Theology in the Anglican Communion*.